The Garden Book

WITH ILLUSTRATIONS FROM THE COLLECTION OF THE
MUSEUM OF FINE ARTS, BOSTON

BRACKEN BOOKS

LONDON

ILLUSTRATIONS

Niels Emil Severin Holm
VIEW OF THE STRAITS OF MESSINA FROM A COUNTRY HOUSE
1859
oil on canvas
32½ × 51½"
Tompkins Collection; Gift of John Goelet

John Singer Sargent
VILLA DI MARLIA: A FOUNTAIN
1910
watercolor
16 × 20¾"
Hayden Collection. Charles Henry Hayden Fund

Sir Lawrence Alma-Tadema
WOMAN AND FLOWERS
1868
oil on panel
19⅝ × 14⅝"
Gift of Edward Jackson Holmes

Emil Nolde
IRIS
20th-century
watercolor
18½ × 13½"
Seth K. Sweetser Fund

John Sloan
FLOWERS IN SPRING
c. 1920
oil on canvas
30 × 25"
Gift of Amelia E. White

Ross Sterling Turner
A GARDEN IS A SEA OF FLOWERS
1912
watercolor
20½ × 30½"
Gift of the estate of Nellie P. Carter

Jean François Millet
POTATO PLANTERS
19th-century
oil on canvas
32½ × 39⅞"
Gift of Quincy Adams Shaw through Quincy A. Shaw, Jr. and Mrs. Marian Shaw Haughton

Mary Stevenson Cassatt
GATHERING FRUIT
c. 1893
drypoint and aquatint in color
16¾ × 11¾"
Gift of William Emerson and Charles Henry Hayden Fund

Gustave Caillebotte
FRUIT DISPLAYED ON A STAND
19th-century
oil on canvas
30⅛ × 39⅝"
Fanny P. Mason Fund in Memory of Alice Thevin

Chao Shu-ju
SUMMER BLOSSOMS
1926
ink and color on paper
44¾ × 19⅝"
Keith McLeod Fund

John La Farge
APPLE BLOSSOMS
19th-century
watercolor
10⅙ × 7⅝"
Bequest of Mrs. Henry Lee Higginson

Claude Monet
WATER LILIES (I)
1905
oil on canvas
35¼ × 39½"
Gift of Edward Jackson Holmes

Anonymous
WILSON'S ALBANY (STRAWBERRIES) from D.M. Dewey's NURSERYMAN'S POCKET BOOK OF SPECIMEN FRUIT AND FLOWERS
1875
stencil and watercolor
8¾ × 5¼"
Gift of Mrs. Alan Tawse

Joseph Stella
CACTUS AND TROPICAL FOLIAGE
c. 1922
watercolor over graphite
18⅛ × 24⅛"
Sophie M. Friedman Fund

French or Franco-Flemish
NARCISSUS from Ovid's *METAMORPHOSES*
late 15th- or early 16th-century
tapestry; wool and silk
111 × 122½"
Charles Potter Kling Fund

The Garden Book is published by Bracken Books
a division of Bestseller Publications Ltd.,
Princess House, 50 East Castle Street,
London W1N 7AP, England

Printed in Spain.

ISBN 1 85170 222 9 (Standard edition)
ISBN 1 85170 235 0 (Deluxe edition)

Contents

Foreword

Through gardening we are given
the key to some of Nature's most
inspiring secrets; and as we work
together with the elements to
raise flowers, fruits, and vegetables,
we are permitted to catch many a
glimpse of Nature's miracles and
we are given many of her gifts.

In these pages you can record the
pleasures of your gardening year.
This book will store these facts,
and in these notes your garden will
be in bloom at all seasons and for
all time.

*No occupation is as delightful to me
as the culture of the earth, and no
culture comparable to that of the garden*

Thomas Jefferson

This is the garden of

Mary Baxter Mackintosh

Sandee Baxter Mackintosh

Sinclair Mackintosh

Its location is

Havedore, Dornoch, Sutherland, Y

It specializes in

Rockery Plants

Wild Flowers

Shrubs

VIEW OF THE STRAITS OF MESSINA FROM A COUNTRY HOUSE—Niels Emil Severin Holm

My Garden

There is a garden…
Where roses and white lilies grow;
A heavenly paradise is that place.'

Thomas Campion

History

Date started ___ 1988 August

Size ___ 3/4 Acre

Type of soil ___ Variable

Climate ___ Moderate ~~XXX~~

Light ___ Good

Past Plantings of Note

Perennials ___ planted 1988 house unoccupied from

1973-1988 no guardining done then

Shrubs and trees ___ H~~XXXXXX~~ planted cypress in

aprox 1947 and converted playing fields into a shrubery

Bulbs ___ ~~XXXXXXXXXXXX~~

Annuals

VILLA DI MARLIA: A FOUNTAIN—John Singer Sargent

My Flower Garden

*Men plant flowers because it represents
a way of affirming the renewability of life—
watching them grow each year, you know
you can do it again next year.* Anonymous

Future Plantings and Projects
Hopes and Goals

My Flower Garden

Long before [man] existed the land was in fact regularly plowed, and still continues to be thus plowed, by earthworms.   Charles Darwin

Fertilizers

Types

Where applied

_____

_____

_____

_____

_____

Dates applied

_____

_____

_____

_____

My Flower Garden

God Almighty first planted a garden

Sir Francis Bacon

Seeds Ordered or Purchased

Type of seed   Ordered from

_____   _____

_____   _____

_____   _____

_____   _____

_____   _____

_____   _____

Comments

_____

_____

_____

_____

IRIS—Emil Nolde

My Flower Garden

Short of Aphrodite, there is nothing
lovelier on this planet than a flower.

Peter Tompkins

Flowers Planted—Annuals

Started indoors   Date

_____

_____

Planted outdoors   Location

_____

_____

Purchased in boxes   Source

_____

_____

Biennials

How started   Date started   Source

_____

_____

FLOWERS IN SPRING—John Sloan

A man of words and not of deeds,
Is like a garden full of weeds.

Mother Goose

Weeding Schedule

Sweet April showers
Do spring May flowers.

Thomas Tusser

Watering Schedule

My Flower Garden

How does the meadow flower its bloom unfold?
Because the lovely little flower is free
Down to its roots, and, in that freedom, bold.

William Wordsworth

Flowering Record

Flower   Date

_____   _____

_____   _____

_____   _____

_____   _____

_____   _____

_____   _____

_____   _____

_____   _____

_____   _____

_____   _____

A GARDEN IS A SEA OF FLOWERS—Ross Sterling Turner

My Flower Garden

Shed no tear! O shed no tear!
The flower will bloom another year!
Weep no more! Weep no more!
Young buds sleep in the root's white core.

John Keats

Storage of Bulbs,
Corms and Tender Plants

Type	How & where stored
Tulip Bulbs	Dry in coal cellar

My Flower Garden

Everything that grows,
Holds in perfection but a little moment.

William Shakespeare

Miscellaneous Notes

Aug 1991 - got a box of Geraniume & others from

Joan Carford

Ragged Robin (3')

Geranium Macrotrhizium (Album?) 2' - very fragrant

True Catmint

Geranium Sanquinum ⎤ 2 low growing prostate ones
   v Ballerina   ⎦ in MB's rockery

Geranium Dalmaticum - ~~MB's rockery~~

Geranium Kashmir white (Disappears in winter)
            so remember where it is
            by MB's wall

My Vegetable, Fruit & Herb Garden

The earth bringeth forth fruit of herself:
first the blade, then the ear, after that
the full corn in the ear.' Mark 4:28

Soil Preparation

_____

_____

_____

_____

_____

_____

_____

_____

_____

_____

_____

POTATO PLANTERS—Jean François Millet

To own a bit of ground, to scratch it with a hoe,
to plant seeds, and watch the renewal of life—
this is the commonest delight of the race,
the most satisfactory thing a man can do.

Charles Dudley Warner

Seed Sowing

Started indoors	Date	Source

Sown in the garden

Comments

_____

_____

My Vegetable, Fruit & Herb Garden

Draw the layout here

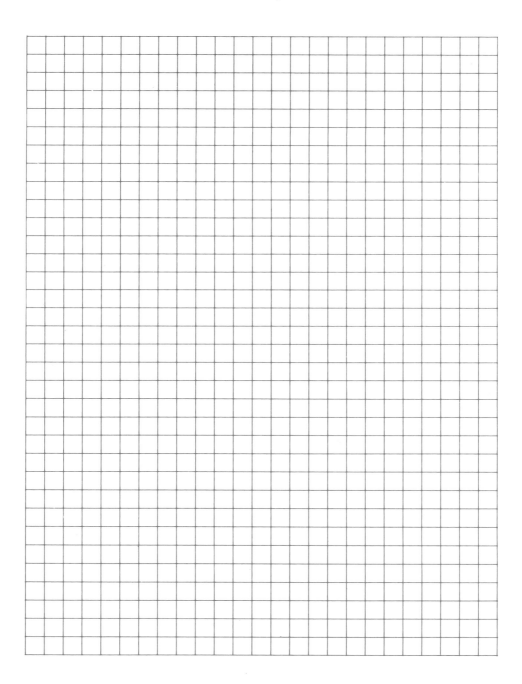

All the fruits will outdo what the
flowers have started.

François de Malherbe

Transplanting, pruning, staking, etc.

_____

_____

_____

_____

_____

_____

_____

_____

Comments

_____

_____

_____

_____

GATHERING FRUIT—*Mary Stevenson Cassatt*

Long about knee deep in June;
'Bout the time Strawberries melts
On the vine.
James Whitcomb Riley

Fertilizing Schedule

Who loves a garden still his Eden keeps,
Perennial pleasures, plants, and wholesome
harvest reaps.
Amos Bronson Alcott

Mulching, Weeding and Watering Schedule

_____

_____

_____

_____

_____

_____

_____

_____

_____

_____

_____

_____

_____

Training is everything. The peach was once a bitter almond; cauliflower is nothing but a cabbage with a college education.

Mark Twain

The Harvest

Date	What	Quantity	Comments

FRUIT DISPLAYED ON A STAND—Gustave Caillebotte

My Vegetable, Fruit & Herb Garden

Much pleasure we have lost,' while we abstained
From the delightful fruit,' nor known til now,
True relish, tasting.

John Milton

Bottling, Preserving, Freezing and Drying

Date	What	Quantity	Comments

The first cuckoo of the year provokes a silent prayer, as also the first asparagus and the first green pea.

Harold Nicolson

Miscellaneous Notes

Holy Mother Earth, the trees and all nature
are witnesses of your thoughts and deeds.

Winnebago Indian Saying

Extant Plantings and Future Plans

_____

_____

_____

_____

_____

_____

_____

_____

_____

_____

_____

_____

_____

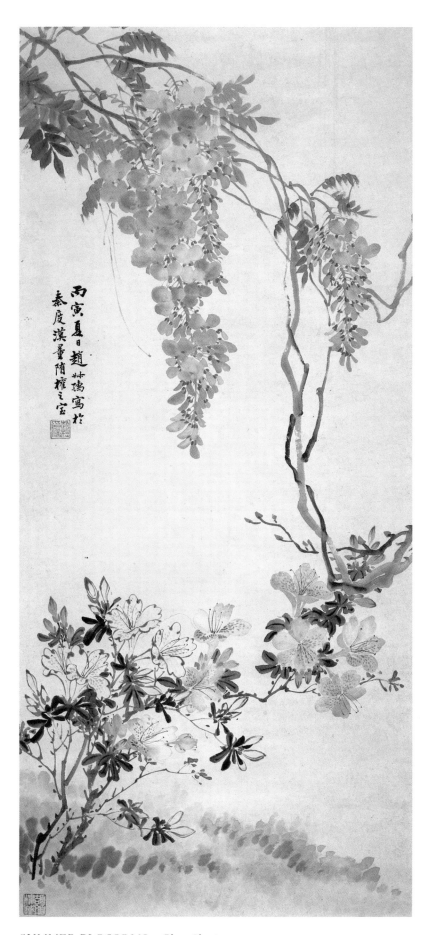

SUMMER BLOSSOMS—Chao Shu-ju

My Lawn

Like snow, dandelions enchant children
but dismay adults.   Barbara Pond

Fertilizing   Date

_____   _____

_____   _____

_____   _____

Weed control

_____   _____

_____   _____

_____   _____

Mowing schedule

_____   _____

_____   _____

_____   _____

My Trees & Shrubs

*I believe a leaf of grass is no less
than the journey-work of the stars.*

Walt Whitman

New Plantings

Types   Location

_____   _____

_____   _____

_____   _____

_____   _____

_____   _____

_____   _____

_____   _____

Comments

_____

_____

My Trees & Shrubs

Myriads of rivulets running through the lawn,
The moan of doves in the immemorial elms
And murmuring of innumerable bees.

Alfred Lord Tennyson

Pruning, Fertilizing and Watering Schedule

Task   Date

_____   _____

_____   _____

_____   _____

_____   _____

_____   _____

_____   _____

_____   _____

_____   _____

_____   _____

_____   _____

APPLE BLOSSOMS—John La Farge

Weather

O farmers, pray that your summers
be wet and your winters clear
Virgil

First frost

_____

_____

_____

Last frost

_____

_____

_____

Heat spells

_____

_____

_____

_____

Rainfall and dry spells

_____

_____

_____

_____

_____

Weather

Now the summer came to pass,
And the flowers through the grass
Joyously sprang,
While all the tribes of birds sang.

Walther von der Vogelweide

Miscellaneous Notes and Comments

Miscellaneous Purchases

We must cultivate our garden

Voltaire

Date	Item	Cost	Comments

WATER LILIES (I)—Claude Monet

Joy...entices flowers from seeds,
Suns from the firmament.

Friedrich von Schiller

Draw your plan here

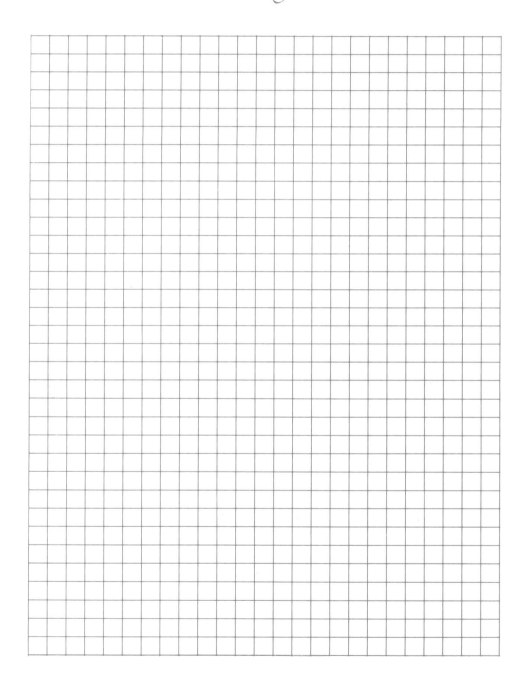

Spring, the sweet spring, is the year's
pleasant king;
Then blooms each thing...
Cold doth not sting, the pretty birds do sing...

Thomas Nashe

WILSON'S ALBANY.

Hardy, productive.

AMERICAN

WILSON'S ALBANY (STRAWBERRIES)—*Anonymous*

Visits to Special Gardens

I know a bank whereon the wild thyme blows,
Where oxlips and the nodding violet grows
Quite overcanopied with luscious woodbine,
With sweet musk-roses and with eglantine.

William Shakespeare

Garden _____

Location _____

Date visited _____

Plantings of interest & good ideas _____

_____

Comments _____

_____

Garden _____

Location _____

Date visited _____

Plantings of interest & good ideas _____

_____

Comments _____

_____

*Consider the lilies of the field, how they grow;
they toil not, neither do they spin... even
Solomon in all his glory was not arrayed like
one of these.*

Matthew 6:28-29

Garden _____

Location _____

Date visited _____

Plantings of interest & good ideas _____

_____

Comments _____

_____

Garden _____

Location _____

Date visited _____

Plantings of interest & good ideas _____

_____

Comments _____

_____

Rose is a rose is a rose is a rose.

Gertrude Stein

Additional Notes and Comments

_____

_____

_____

_____

_____

_____

_____

_____

_____

_____

_____

_____

_____

CACTUS AND TROPICAL FOLIAGE—Joseph Stella

Garden Photographs

Garden Lore

No one knows
Through what wild centuries
Roves back the rose.

Walter de la Mare

Unusual and Helpful Garden Lore
I Have Learned or Read

NARCISSUS—French or Franco-Flemish

My Favourite Garden Books

Title _____
Author _____
Comments _____
_____

Title _____
Author _____
Comments _____
_____

Title _____
Author _____
Comments _____
_____

Title _____
Author _____
Comments _____
_____

Checklist of Supplies

Mulch
Peat moss
Potting soil
Sand
Vermiculite or Perlite
Leafmold or compost
Manure
Organic fertilizer
Inorganic fertilizer
Boxes
Clay pots
Peat pots for seedlings
Labels
Waterproof marking pens
Chicken wire
Burlap
Plastic sheeting
Stakes
Twine
Twisters
Rubbish bags
Gloves
Cultivating rake
Leaf and/or grass rake
Hoe
Digging spade

Weeder/cultivator
Border fork
Bulb planter
Trowel
Cutting shears
Grass shears
Hedge shears
Lawnmower
Power saw
Wheelbarrow
Secateurs
Watering can
Hose
Sprinkler attachments
5-gallon plastic pails
Miscellaneous:

_____

_____

_____

_____

_____

_____

Addresses & Telephone Numbers

Nurseries; Seed, Plant and Bulb Sources;
Garden Centres and Garden Supply Sources;
Garden Clubs and Organizations;
Lawn Care; etc.

64